Leisure Arts 11

Portraits in Pastel

Dennis Frost

SEARCH PRESS

Wellwood North Farm Road Tunbridge Wells

Introduction

Pastel can produce very subtle tones or colours, though it has an earthy quality; it has a wonderful fluidity, yet each stroke, whether quick or slow, has permanence and weight. Above all, pastel can give rhythm and a special vibrancy of colour.

Pastel has to be used with care and skill if you want to exploit its best qualities. A stick of pastel sharpened and used end-on will produce a strong, narrow line. Break a stick in half, use it on its side and a wide grainy stroke covers the paper.

You can obtain a range of effects between these two extremes by varying the *size* of the piece used and the *pressure* with which it is applied to the paper.

Once the pastel is on the paper, its character can be totally changed by rubbing. This technique is controversial, but if rubbing achieves the desired effect, it seems justifiable. Superb works in pastel have been produced both with and without rubbing.

I do a lot of rubbing in the early stages of a pastel to create the right colour, tone and balance. In the final stages of the work, I apply the pastel in firm, decisive strokes on top of underworking, to give an effect of spontaneity and vigour. I use the side of my little finger to change the shape, texture or weight of a pastel mark. I find it is more sensitive than any paper stump that is available for this purpose, though somewhat messier. If you use the rubbing technique, remove excess pastel dust by blowing on the paper while you are working. I work with my board upright and find it disconcerting when dark pastel dust descends from the upper to the lower part of the work. Vigorous and regular blowing is essential when working in pastel.

Materials

I use a well-known make of pastels that are distinguishable by the numbering system used to grade the weight of colour. For example, in 'poppy red 6', the six denotes the tint value. However, these particular pastels are quite soft and I also use a few of a harder brand.

The early stages of these demonstrations were drawn with conté sticks; I also used them to redefine the drawing in the final stages of some examples.

Pastels tossed into a tray while you are working soon become grubby. Keep a separate tray or a large, deep tin filled with about 50 mm (2 in) of cooking rice. At the end of the day, drop the used pastels into this and agitate for a few minutes until they are clean and ready for re-use.

I used an inexpensive paper, Canson Ingres, for all the examples in this book. It has a surface (tooth) which is sufficiently textured to hold the pastel adequately. Tint 55 was suitable for nearly all the subjects.

If you make a bad mistake, use a putty eraser to lift off some areas of pastel. A pencil eraser will remove conté drawing. My most useful erasing-tool is a 50 mm (2 in) flat varnish-brush with which I lightly dust the paper. This removes only the surface pastel; whatever is engrained into the paper tooth remains but is so slight that it is usually obliterated during reworking.

You do not need much equipment for work with pastels. To begin with, buy:
a rigid easel,
a large drawing-board, approximately 375 × 550 mm (15 × 22 in),
several sheets of paper, clipped to the board to provide a cushion for the top sheet of pastel paper,
a tray for the pastels,
a wet and a dry cloth for wiping hands,
a tin or jar of rice for cleaning pastels,
a dust sheet to cover the floor.

Fixing pastels

I rarely fix pastels. I wish the last statement of colour and tone to be mine and not altered indiscriminately by a medium that changes tone and colour very unevenly.

A fixative drastically alters a pastel portrait worked in extremely subtle tones. Moreover, I have found that after fixing a work (and losing some of the quality in the process), the portrait is not completely fixed and can still be smudged quite easily.

In my opinion, a work is best preserved by framing and glazing it. This is expensive, unless you go to the trouble of making your own frames. Before framing a pastel, hold it up between finger and thumb in one hand and tap the back of the paper to remove loose particles of pastel. Do this until no dust is left. You must use a mount when framing. A carefully-chosen colour will bring out the best in your work and separate the painting from the glass. Otherwise dust might be transferred to the glass and cause unsightly shadows and smears. You can cut a bevelled edge on the inside edge of a mount; this needs practice but is worth the effort.

Heat-sealing is another way of preserving work. This technique is used commercially to protect prints; a transparent sheet of thin plastic covers the painting and is sealed directly on to it under heat and pressure. It is not entirely successful, for some tonal alteration is unavoidable with fixing. However, I have had several life-drawings in pastel treated in this way and then mounted directly on to a chipboard base, with the overall effect of a print. I do not consider this a suitable method of preserving a work of any importance.

Making your own pastels

This is not necessary unless you are dissatisfied with the pastels available commercially, or wish to know how pastels are made.

To make a pastel you need:
colour,
gum tragacanth
white chalk,
water.

Grind the colour to a very fine powder and saturate it with water to which gum tragacanth has been added. Grind some white chalk as finely as possible and treat in the same way as the colour. Mix the two together, varying the proportions according to the tint you require. Blend the two substances and allow them to settle so that surplus moisture may be poured off. Put the remainder in a bag of close-weave material and squeeze. Knead the remaining paste until it is plastic in consistency, then shape it into sticks. Allow these to dry completely; then they are ready for use.

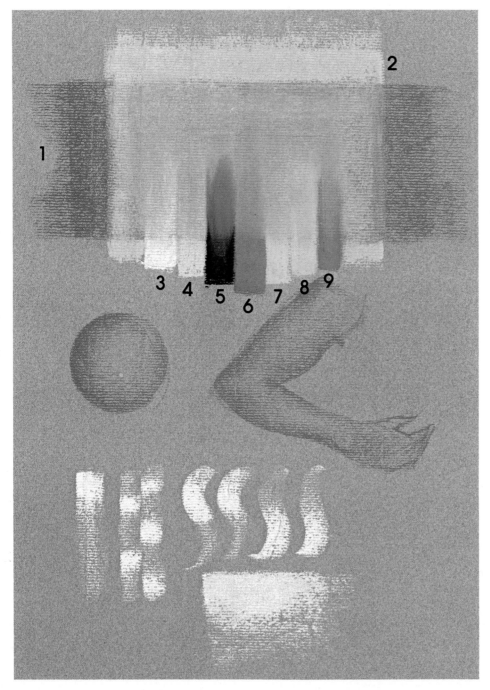

Flesh tones

I use these nine colours for all my portraits. I make the basic flesh tone by superimposing madder brown O over sanguine conté (colour 2 over colour 1). I use the other colours to indicate flesh under varying conditions of light and shadow.

1 sanguine conté
2 madder brown O
3 silver white
4 Naples yellow 2
5 Vandyke brown 8
6 poppy red 6
7 lizard green 3
8 Prussian blue 1
9 blue grey 4

I drew the arm and ball with a short piece of sanguine conté used on its side. I indicated the form by varying the pressure of the stroke. The white strokes below show the extreme changes of tone achieved by the slightest variation of stroke pressure. If you are a beginner, practise this until you begin to develop a 'feel' for pastel.

Hair

I find these colours useful for most hair:

1 black
2 blue grey 6
3 Prussian blue 1
4 Vandyke brown 8
5 Vandyke brown 6
6 Naples yellow 2
7 sanguine conté
8 lemon yellow

The four examples of hair shown here are a base for an infinite variety of colourings. I work from the darkest to the lightest tone, rubbing occasionally to create in-between tones and the more subtle colours.

I painted the blonde hair on the lower right by blocking in the whole area with Vandyke brown 6, taking care not to use too much pressure. Next, I applied some sanguine conté to the parts of the hair that were lighter in tone and then did the same exercise with Naples yellow 2. Finally, I applied the highlights with lemon yellow 2. Note that highlights can be small areas of the brightest colour.

Painting children

Most of my commissioned works are portraits of children; they are very satisfying to complete. The most difficult part is to try to persuade a child between two and five years of age to sit still for more than a few moments. If you talk to a little child, he or she will look straight at you, giving a full-face pose. Ask someone to talk to the child from the side and you have a profile. Little children are most still when being read to, watching television or just fast asleep. You will have to take your chance when it comes unless you are an extremely fast worker.

Facial expressions

A common criticism of a finished portrait is the lack of a broad smile, for a face in repose has a serious expression. A camera can record the broadest smile in a fraction of a second, but a sitter cannot be expected to hold a smile for longer than a few minutes. To capture any momentary expression, learn to study a face and remember its details once the individual has gone.

You cannot render a natural expression by drawing a smile only on the mouth. Study your own smile in a mirror and then watch the changes in musculature as you let the smile relax. When you smile, the eyes narrow and little pouches appear beneath them. The distance from below the nose to the top lip diminishes, the mouth widens and the cheeks become more rounded, which in turn widens the nostrils. The whole structure of the face alters.

Painting from photographs

There is nothing wrong with painting from photographs, though purists insist that all drawing and painting must be done from life. If you use a photograph as a source for a portrait, strive for a result with a 'painterly' quality, rather than slavishly copy the print. The aim of working in pastel is to interpret a subject and say: 'This is how *I* see it'.

For some subjects photographs are the only sources of reference; they are invaluable for wild life, foreign places and so on.

Although I do most of my work from life, I have worked from old, poor-quality or black-and-white photographs. I find it a challenge to produce a picture that looks like a painting.

Keep a scrap-book as a source of reference. I collect pictures of people, places and figures that have caught my attention. I have referred back to almost every one of them at some time over the years.

Points to remember

Four drawing techniques specific to pastel give more style, rhythm and success to every work. They are:

Pressure of stroke – the length of pastel stick and the weight with which you apply it determine the character of the line produced.

Rubbing – how you shape a pastel mark once it is on the paper makes a vast difference to its visual effect.

Lost and found – it is far more effective to insinuate an edge (such as the profile of a face or a hairline) than to draw it as one hard, mechanical line. Read the caption to stage 4 of the painting on page 16.

Overstatement – it is sometimes necessary to overstate a colour to produce the right effect. Knowing when to do this comes with experience.

Painting mouths

The mouth at the top left on page 8 illustrates the basic colours used on the other three. To draw the mouth on the top right, begin by indicating the top lip and edge of lips with bistre conté, as is just visible on the mouth at the top left of the page. Use sanguine conté over the areas of lips and flesh and then overpaint with madder brown O. Rub these colours together to produce a subtle blend of tones. Now indicate the lips with poppy red 6 and put in the teeth with silver white. Place dark areas of shadow behind the teeth with black conté and use a little blue grey 4 for the lighter shadows on the teeth on the left. Add flesh highlights with madder brown O and put in tiny grooves on the lips with conté sharpened to a fine point to give texture.

The two other mouths on page 8 are variations on the same theme. Use the same procedure.

Painting eyes

For the sake of demonstration, the four eyes on page 9 are shown in various stages of development.

Begin by drawing the eye on the top left with bistre conté. Then add blue grey 4 and blue grey 6 as shown at the top right. On the lower left, outline the iris and pupil in black conté and use indigo 1 and blue grey 4 for the white of the eyes (which I never paint plain white, lest it appear too stark). If you study a baby's eyes, you will notice that the eyes are quite blue and nowhere near white.

To complete the eye, rub the indigo 1 over the edge of the blue grey 4 so that it is the dominant colour. Give form to the iris, darken it with blue grey 6, and add tiny touches of light with indigo 1. Put in the point of reflected light with Rembrandt white, and mark a dash of poppy red 6 in the corner of the eye.

The tonal values for the skin surrounding the eye are equal in strength to, or lighter than, the white of the eye, except where there are dark shadowy areas.

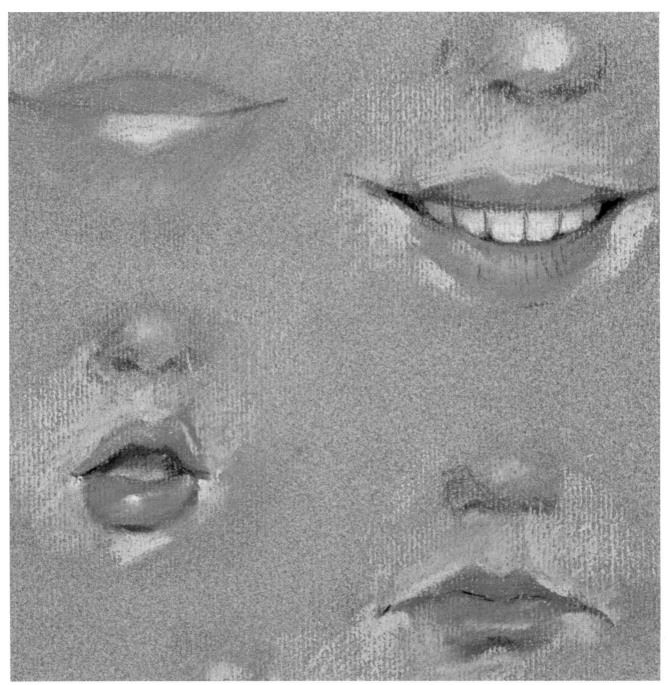

Painting mouths

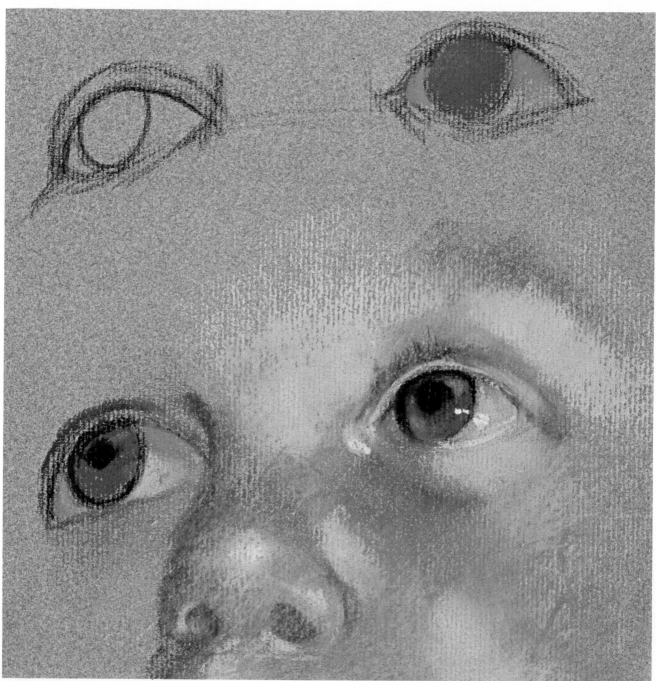

Painting eyes

Emma: demonstration

I find profiles are the easiest portraits to complete. There is no problem such as a full or three-quarter view that requires a foreshortened nose, or a mouth and lips needing a fulness that can only be described by tone. But profiles do have problems of their own, especially when drawing the eye. Unless you study the shapes carefully, an interpretation can look wrong and disappoint you.

To give this demonstration interest, I asked Emma to tilt her head forward so that the painting became more than a mere silhouette. An alternative would have been to turn the body towards me while keeping the head in profile.

Stage 1

As always with children, I had to work fairly fast, so that I had made a good start when Emma's concentration waned. I sketched the profile with black conté, making sure that the head, neck and shoulders were outlined correctly. For the sake of this demonstration, I centred the head in the picture. Usually I allow more space for the face to look into than at the back of the head.

Stage 2

I began to build up tone, using madder brown 8 for the shadows and white for the hair, ribbon and clothes. I made all these marks with the side of the pastel stick to avoid a too specific effect at this stage. Next, I added a little colour: poppy red 6 in the ear and eye shadow, green grey 4 into the background and a little cobalt blue O in front of the face. I rubbed the flesh tones, made with madder brown O, on the cheek and nose. I also diffused the density of the pastel on the eye, ear and dress with my little finger.

Stage 3

In stage 2, I established the hair tone and in this stage I gave the hair its colour values with Vandyke brown 8, black and lemon yellow 4. I used black sparingly for the darkest areas at the back of the hair and at the front of the fringe. I rubbed in lemon yellow 4 to give the right amount of highlight.

I built up the flesh tones by blending more madder brown O, and poppy red 6, using rubbing rather than too much pastel to create the right density. A little blue grey 4 introduced to the nose and mouth area gave recession and shadow when rubbed. I defined the shape of the eye with black conté and did the same to the ear, chin and jaw with Vandyke brown 8.

I found the tonal values at this stage of the work a little out-of-balance. The portrait appeared 'top-heavy' because of the dark mass of hair and the lack of weight in the dress and shoulder. I consider my work as a series of corrections that diminish to the point where I am satisfied that each problem has been confronted, studied and solved.

Stage 4

My concern at this stage was to refine the portrait. I worked some green grey 6 into the hair to reinforce the shadows and then overpainted with Naples yellow 2 to suggest highlights and direction in the hair. I made these marks with the side of the pastel and used more pressure in the middle of the stroke than at the ends.

I put a touch of cobalt blue O into the cheekbone and on the background before the face to emphasize the profile more. To create the illusion of more space before Emma than behind her, I added grass green 1 to the lower left-hand corner and green grey 4 to the top right.

Stage 5

Although the portrait was nearly finished, much tonal adjustment was still needed. I used a 25 mm (1 in) piece of sanguine conté on its side to add warmth to the hair, then skimmed as lightly as possible over the top with silver white to give a glazed effect.

Moving down to the face, I applied poppy red 6 lightly over the eye area, cheek and chin to give a less harsh effect. I 'broke' the hard line of the nose and mouth by dragging the pastel on the face and that on the background into one another. Almost the entire difference between the flesh tones in stages 4 and 5 was produced by rubbing in. I diffused one tone or colour into another with the side of my little finger; no more colour was added to the paper: all I did was to redistribute colour that was already there. I put a mass of cobalt blue O in front of the face to sharpen the profile without using any strong colour or harsh line.

For the dress I worked Rembrandt pastel over the original silver white mass of the dress and ribbon. I dragged some of the flesh tones into the cloth on the back of the shoulder and then put in the shadows on the sleeve and ribbon with blue grey 4.

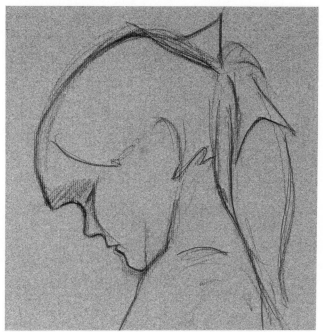

Stage 1

Detail

There are no definite hard edges in or around the eye. The strong profile shape hardly has a line in it; it is composed mainly of 'dots' of colour.

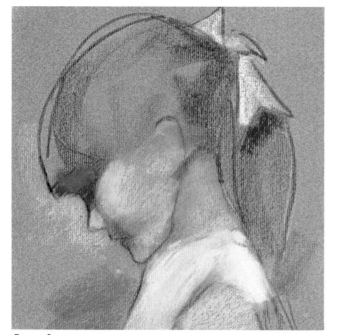

Stage 2

Stage 3

Stage 4

Stage 5 – the finished painting

Detail from the finished painting on page 12

Boy fishing: demonstration

One weekend I visited an old mill not far from my home. There was a wide stretch of water beside it and some boys were fishing there. It had rained recently, the river was quite swollen and the boys seemed to be concentrating more than they usually do when in a group. Each was watching the float and ready to strike at the slightest twitch or tug of a fish. Luckily, I had my pencils with me so I made some action studies of these lads.

Stage 1

I studied the sketches I had made and decided to choose one with a high eye-level because I felt that a horizon of stream or bank did not help the composition.

I made a tentative light drawing in black conté, taking great care with the proportions. When they were reasonably accurate, I used compressed charcoal boldly, to strengthen some of the most important lines.

Then I studied the original sketches made at the mill and began to work in the darkest tonal areas with a 25 mm (1 in) long piece of madder brown 8 used on its side. I think only in terms of tone at this stage of a drawing, as I consider the balance of darks and lights to be most important for a successful study.

Stage 2

As the sun was bright and the water lively, I decided to be vigorous throughout the preliminary stages of this sketch, knowing I could always mute the more strident areas later by lightly dusting them with a flat 50 mm (2 in) varnish-brush that I use just for this purpose.

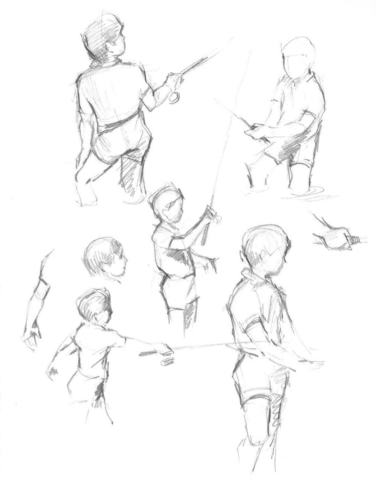

I began to give mass to the figure by using a piece of Prussian blue 8 on its side. I used Vandyke brown 6 and viridian 6 on their sides for the hair and rubbed them in a little with my finger to give depth. The viridian 6 added at this stage is used purely as an undercolour; although it hardly shows in the finished drawing, its presence is detectable. The cool colours on the head gave a basis for recession so that the warm colours to be added to the highlights later would stand out. I laid in the neck, arms and legs with a flesh tone made from madder brown O and poppy red 6, making no attempt at final colour but concentrating on tonal weight and overall balance in the work.

I added a little silver white on its side as a high tone and then used its sharp edge to denote *direction* of form rather than form itself.

Stage 3

Satisfied that the basic lines and tones were correct, I began to work up the form and colour. I added darker tones to the hair and a light tone to the crown to give form. I introduced poppy red 6 to the ear area, then blocked in the shirt tones with silver white and cobalt blue 2, using the latter colour for the shorts as well. As the boy was dressed in cool colours and only the flesh tints were warm, the choice of background was critical. I laid in cobalt blue 2, silver white and sap green 3, but these appeared too strong so I toned them down in the final painting. I used cobalt blue 2 and silver white quite heavily around the head so that the profile became more pronounced.

Stage 4

To produce the effect of swirling water, I overpainted the background with silver white, madder brown O, Naples yellow 2, viridian 3 and lemon yellow 4 to make up the water. Note that these are not 'water' colours but give a powerful impression. The shadow on the lower right of the painting echoed the dark area on the shirt and gave depth to the water. I was still unconvinced by the background, so I added a few curved strokes of Prussian blue 1 and blue grey 14, which gave more substance to the water.

I began the final work on the figure by overworking the head highlights with the sides of silver white and blue grey 4. When adding highlights, I used varying pressure on each stroke so that a whiter highlight was produced by applying a slightly harder pressure at the end of the movement. The edge of the hair at the top of the head is not a continuous line but is 'lost-and-found': the tonal change is only *insinuated* by the preceding and following white line. This is also noticeable on the left forearm on page 17.

I rubbed poppy red 6 on the cheek to create shadow, and modified the dark area dividing the head and neck to give continuous tone and tilt the head further away.

I reduced the harsh drawing in the arm by rubbing and gentle overwork to describe the soft flesh. I used poppy red 6 and blue grey 4 for the the mauve shadows on the right forearm and left leg.

Detail

Outlines were accentuated in some areas by differences in tonal value. This is apparent on the left arm: the 'lost-and-found' technique described in stage 4. The fishing-reel was painted scrappily but looked realistic in the finished painting. There were no specific details in the hands, just colour changes and varying tones.

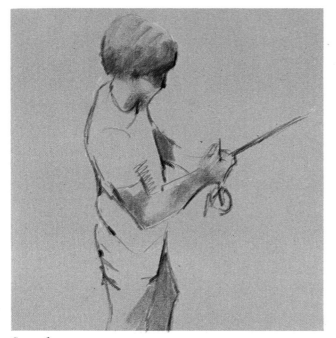

Stage 1

Stage 2

Stage 3

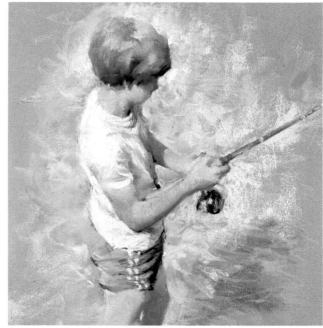

Stage 4 – the finished painting

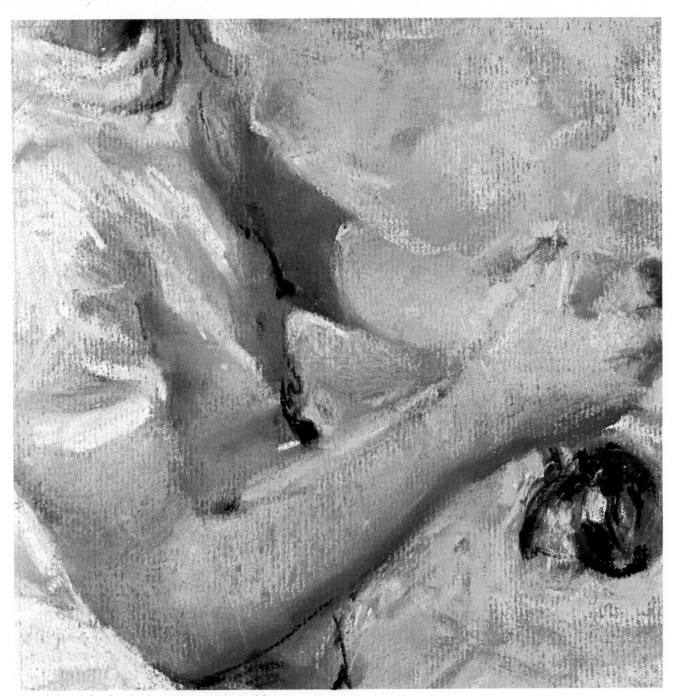

Detail from the finished painting on page 16

Nude: demonstration

Painting nudes is a great challenge as mistakes or a phlegmatic approach show very clearly. I find a bold attitude is essential but this does not necessarily mean using bold lines or colours. This demonstration is a strong drawing, but has sensitivity, which is what I aim for.

I find that the 'perfect' figure is not the most inspiring to draw or paint as there are fewer difficulties or new problems to be solved. The subtle tones of muscular variation in the back of this young girl make an interesting exercise in painting flesh.

Stage 1

I used black conté to outline the figure and establish the position and proportions. Conté is the ideal medium for this preliminary work as it can be erased at this stage or overpainted with pastel later. Then I strengthened the main structural lines and shadow areas with compressed charcoal. Notice that I have slightly changed the sitting angle from the position in the original drawing.

I made this sketch in about 15 minutes at an evening life class. It breaks down into four clear working-methods, as follows. First I made a simple line-drawing in pastel, purely to map out the proportions. Then I blocked the darkest areas of tone and rubbed the edges of these areas to give softer parts. Next I reinforced the form by adding highlights, and finally redefined the original drawing in some parts, using black conté to accentuate just a few edges and give rhythm to the figure.

Stage 2

I began to give the figure solidity by adding the darkest tonal areas in madder brown 8, used on its side. I rubbed these slightly to soften some of the hard edges. To begin with, I exaggerated each tonal value so that the relative tonal values were clearly defined and I was sure that they were correct. It was easy to diminish their strength later.

Stage 3

I used a restricted 'palette' in these early stages so that I concentrated on tones and kept distracting colours to a minimum. I reduced the strength of the darker areas with madder brown O. To make this effective and give variety to the strokes, I broke a stick of pastel to about 18 mm (¾ in) and used it lightly on its side over the whole figure, applying more pressure where I wanted highlights. Then I merged the tones into each other by rubbing with the side of my little finger.

I added some Vandyke brown 6 for the hair, making no attempt to create anything other than a soft mass of tone.

Stage 1

Stage 4

I added a white background, letting it run across the edges of the figure and across the upper arms to soften the hard edges. I worked some poppy red 6 into the elbows, cobalt blue 2 and a touch of grass green 4 into the shoulder, neck and waist areas. Although the painting was coming together well, I felt it was still too hard, so I used my 50 mm (2 in) flat varnish-brush to balance and even-up the tones and soften some of the harder edges.

Stage 5

I blocked in the background in a determined manner and took great care with the edges, breaking into some but leaving hard white edges in other places to define a particular curve or angle. I worked into some of the muscle shadows and established a few highlights on the head, elbow and hand. I added Vandyke brown 6 to the lower part of the study to complete tonal and colour balance with the head.

Stage 2

Stage 3

Stage 4

The hair has no definite shape or texture so as not to detract from the figure; in the same way, the face in shadow has been defined by the background. My whole intention with this painting was to show the muscles in repose. I paid special attention to the mid-back area where madder brown 8 shows through a light glazing of madder brown O and poppy red 6. I used light strokes here so that the tooth of the paper gave a grainy texture and an interesting effect.

Detail

Study the reaction of pastel to the tooth of the paper. When rubbed hard, the pastel is pushed into the crevices between each ridge, giving a soft, flat tone. When rubbed lightly, a more grainy texture is apparent and an optical mixing of colours occurs.

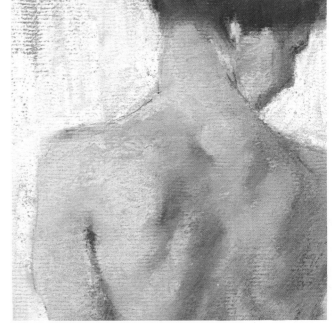

Detail from the finished work on page 21

Stage 5 – the finished work

The library reading room: demonstration

It is hard to find a place where people are still and quiet. It had never occurred to me before that a library might be a place ideally suited to my needs as a portraitist. The old gentleman here had a fine head and features, but I was more struck by his interesting position. He had no moustache, and I decided to add one to soften his rather sharp features. He was completely oblivious of all around him; even the no-smoking sign went unnoticed.

Stage 1

Of the several sketches I made, I found this one most appealing. The way he supported his head with his hand allowed me to make a space at the centre of the picture into which he could look. I used the sharp end of a piece of black conté to set out the drawing and establish the proportions. I found that the composition was more difficult than it seemed, as the arms, back and newspaper formed long bold shapes that had to be balanced carefully.

The head, hands and newspaper were the focal points of this study. I described nearly everything else with Vandyke brown 6, making sweeping strokes with the side of the pastel. Next, I introduced white into the hair, moustache, collar and newspaper as the highlights of the picture. I laid in the preliminary flesh tone with madder brown 0, and used some cadmium yellow 1 on only three areas of the background.

Stage 2

I stopped to study my painting as I was unhappy with the shapes. I decided to change the position of the left hand. I dusted it off then reworked it with madder brown 0 and poppy red 6; this greatly improved the overall composition and made the sweep of the left arm less dramatic.

I went over the figure and restated the darkest areas with compressed charcoal, adding some to the background as well. I find that compressed charcoal is best as it is quite black and does not crumble. I gave some form to the newspaper with silver white, cobalt blue 2 and compressed charcoal: I made no attempt at detail but simply laid in areas of different tonal weight to give an *impression* of printed type and pictures. I built up the background with generous strokes of madder brown 0, cobalt blue 2 and silver white. I worked more colour into the head with a small piece of madder brown 0 to strengthen the highlights. I used poppy red 6 to give prominence to the ear and cheek.

To keep the basic forms clearly defined, I redrew them with black conté, taking care not to let this black line become too dominant.

Stage 3

Now that the overall balance was right, I worked on the flesh tones, building up their form with madder brown 0 on the face and hands. I picked out the highlights in the jaw and temples with cobalt blue 0 and used lemon yellow 2 to denote the sharp highlights across the nose and cheek. These two colours were not present on the face in reality, but if they are used in a pastel in this way, the viewer's eye mixes them to create just the right colour and tone of flesh.

I exaggerated the claw-like hands to enhance the feeling of old age. The flesh tones were satisfactory, so I painted in the spectacles, using cobalt blue 2 for the lens and a little lemon yellow 2 on parts of the frame. Whenever I paint a bespectacled person, I ask him or her to remove them and only replace them when my work is done. To complete the facial detail, I picked out a few highlights with Rembrandt white and black conté.

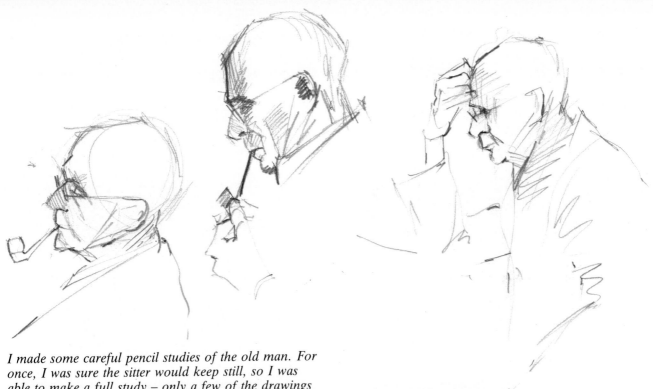

I made some careful pencil studies of the old man. For once, I was sure the sitter would keep still, so I was able to make a full study – only a few of the drawings are reproduced here. His hands were a complete subject on their own. Like many painters, I find hands particularly difficult to draw and so I accepted this challenge with relish.

Now that the flesh colours were substantial, everything else looked incomplete, so I started on the newspaper by rubbing it softly until it was light grey all over. Then I added some dark grey areas to simulate pictures, and shadow under the arm. Lastly, I put in horizontal white lines, using the pastel on its edge. This produced exactly the effect I was hoping for.

I applied Vandyke brown 6 to the suit and rubbed it to give an overall covering. I strengthened the shadows and folds with compressed charcoal and Vandyke brown 8 and I used a little caerulean 2 on the sleeve just below the highlights. The background still needed much work; I added grey green 6 on the right and Vandyke brown 6, olive green 4 and lizard green 8 in the darker background. I arranged these colours around the figure to give maximum contrast: that is, very dark next to very light. Madder brown 0 used with

discretion echoed the flesh tones. The direction of the stroke is important as it can echo or contrast the shape of the figure.

Detail 1

Even though this hand is not particularly well-drawn, it gives a good impression. I used a touch of cobalt blue 2 on the fingertips and wrist.

Detail 2

I overstated the colours of the highlights out-of-context, but these parts are not too prominent when viewed at a distance. Study this detail with a magnifying glass and note the extremes of colour used.

Stage 1

Stage 2

Detail 1

Detail 2

Stage 3 – the finished work

The hairnet: demonstration

I prefer to paint elderly people. It is a joy to try to capture the faded, watery eyes with red rims and the beautifully mauve and purple shadows in the flesh tints. This old lady was on holiday and quite happy to sit and watch younger folk dashing about. Her composure was fascinating and her hairnet and handbag seemed an intrinsic part of her. I wanted to portray a granny with a warm and cheerful personality: someone who had worked hard for a long time and was now enjoying a little relaxation in the sunshine.

I did not place her in any specific background as I wanted no distraction from all the details about her person. There is more space before than behind her, as this gives a more pleasing visual balance.

Stage 1

I began with a black conté sketch but soon realized that a softer approach was necessary, so I changed to bistre conté. The composition was quite simple and I made the preliminary drawing solely to establish the proportions of the figure and the rather round facial features. I was eager to start working with pastels, so I left this drawing understated.

Stage 2

As usual, I began to lay in the darkest tonal areas, using a 25 mm (1 in) piece of Vandyke brown 6 on its side. I also used it on its edge in some places where it was necessary to strengthen lines and the beginnings of detail. I then established the hair with silver white which, as the brightest highlight, gave me a guide to tonal balance. The opposite to this was the dark area of shadow at the back of the head. I was already

pleased with the way this portrait was coming together; I was in no great hurry to complete the work. If I kept the treatment simple, few real problems would arise.

Stage 3

I used terre verte 5 to establish a mid-tone between the dark and light hair tones. At once this produced the first colour that really extended the work. Then I applied the first madder brown 0 to the face and hands to give focal points to the picture. I varied the weight of each pastel stroke to provide variety and tonal contrast.

Stage 1

When I first saw the old lady, I could not decide which viewpoint would provide the more interesting composition, so I made two from different angles. I began to 'get in' to this subject only when I concentrated on her face. The lower drawing made my decision for me.

Stage 2

Stage 3

Stage 4

Detail 1

Stage 5–the finished painting

Stage 4

Then I introduced much more colour, starting with poppy red 6 in the coat where the direction of each stroke was almost as important as the colour itself. I put in the background with Prussian blue 3, madder brown 8, yellow ochre 2 and blue grey 6. I applied this to contrast with the colour and tone of the coat, face and hair. This new pastel had a marked effect on the face as a focal point and I redefined the main features to give more impact, using poppy red 6 on the cheeks and nose and small dashes of Prussian blue 3 near the eye. Facial highlights were put in with short, heavy strokes of madder brown 0. I echoed the background colour by including a little Prussian blue in the hands and hair, rubbing it in well on the latter. Then I added more silver white to the hair, and put in some lines with the sharp end of the pastel stick to indicate the hairnet.

Stage 5

I stood back from my work and assessed its progress. It was (and always is) necessary to relate the background to the figure, and the focal point to the distance. As a general rule, if these parts of the painting progress together the results should be harmonious.

I used lizard green 1, Naples yellow 2, grass green 4 and indigo 1 to lighten the area above the head.

The coat needed much more work. I began by using madder brown 8 for the shadows, poppy red 6 for the mid-tones and madder brown 0 for the highlights. This building up of colour, tone and form was a continual process of applying colour and rubbing it in to achieve the right strength.

I went back to the face and gave the contours extra modelling with my little finger, taking great care to build up the smooth chin, nose and forehead, and to exaggerate the depth of the folds in the flesh around the mouth and eyes. Then, to give a robust effect, I put in the final highlights with firm strokes of a short piece of pastel. I softened parts of the edges of the darker lines to produce gentler, wider areas of colour. Where there was a heavy contrast, I diluted its effect by dragging a nearby lighted colour into it with my finger.

A few more sharp lines of silver white to bring out the hairnet and a dark band around the hair completed the head. Finally, I worked on the handbag and chair, giving special attention to their shiny surfaces. When I next looked at this portrait, I was very satisfied with the result. I felt the approach and handling of pastel looked very 'loose'. By nature, my work tends to be rather tight and I have to make a conscious effort to keep works 'relaxed'. In the previous demonstration, the library reading-room, I indulged myself and allowed the hands, head and newspaper to be much sharper than the rest of the picture.

Detail 1

This shows the swollen, arthritic-looking joints and gnarled hands in detail. There is little drawing; most of the final effect is produced by tonal changes of hard and gentle contrast.

Detail 2 (as shown on back cover)

This shows the face in great detail. You can see almost every pastel stroke, and exactly where and how hard I have used my little finger to achieve the desired tone.

ACKNOWLEDGEMENTS

Portraits in Pastel

Text, drawings and paintings by Dennis Frost.

Text, illustrations, arrangement and typography copyright © Search Press Limited 1981.

First published in Great Britain in 1981 by Search Press Limited, Wellwood, North Farm Road, Tunbridge Wells, Kent TN2 3DR.

Reprinted 1983, 1985, 1987, 1989, 1992

Distributors to the art trade:

UK
Winsor & Newton,
Whitefriars Avenue, Wealdstone,
Harrow, Middlesex HA3 5RH

USA
ColArt Americas Inc.,
11 Constitution Avenue, P. O. Box 1396, Piscataway,
NJ 08855-1396

Arthur Schwartz & Co.,
234 Meads Mountain Road, Woodstock, NY 12498

Canada
Anthes Universal Limited,
341 Heart Lake Road South, Brampton, Ontario L6W 3K8

Australia
Max A. Harrell
P. O. Box 92, Burnley, Victoria 3121

Jasco Pty, Limited
937-941 Victoria Road, West Ryde, N.S.W. 2114

New Zealand
Caldwell Wholesale Limited,
Wellington and Auckland

South Africa
Ashley & Radmore (Pty) Limited,
P. O. Box 2794, Johannesburg 2000

Trade Winds Press (Pty) Limited,
P. O. Box 20194, Durban North 4016

UK ISBN 0 85532 442 2

Made and printed in Spain by A. G. Elkar, S. Coop.
Autonomía, 71 - 48012-Bilbao - Spain.